FINDING YOUR EDGE

Finding YOUR Edge

Building Mental Toughness for Business and Life

Bob Turner

Published by Game Changer Publishing

Paperback ISBN: 978-1-965653-90-6

Hardcover ISBN: 978-1-965653-91-3

Digital ISBN: 978-1-965653-92-0

GC GAME CHANGER
PUBLISHING
www.GameChangerPublishing.com

DEDICATION

This book is dedicated to my parents, Fred & Donna Turner. Without their unconditional love and support, I would have settled for average. Instead, I was taught (and reminded) that the only limits are the ones that we place on ourselves.

Thank you, Mom & Dad.
I am proud to be your son.

READ THIS FIRST

Just to say thanks for buying and reading my book,
I would like to offer you a free 30-minute strategy session,
no strings attached!

Scan the QR Code Here:

SCAN ME

ACKNOWLEDGMENTS

"When I think of Bob Turner, I think of someone who consistently lives on the edge of excellence. His book, *Finding YOUR Edge,* is a reflection of his unwavering commitment to personal and professional growth. Bob challenges you to dig deep, face discomfort head-on, and discover your true potential. This book isn't just a guide—it's a wake-up call to live your best life."

– Ben Newman
USA Today TOP 5 Mindset & Performance Coach
2x Wall Street Journal Bestseller

"In knowing Bob for 25 years, we've shared several of life's milestones. We've seen each other at the high points and shared the lowest lows. He personally was there for me during a very low point in my life when others weren't, and through his guidance and support, I was able to redirect and take charge. He was instrumental in providing a community of positivity and helping me refocus my situation to right the ship. Having competed with

Bob in many endurance races, I've always been amazed at this extra gear he is able to find, allowing himself to push beyond the limits into a place many will never allow themselves to go. *Finding YOUR Edge* is a perfect embodiment of the fire Bob has deep within himself and how he turns up the heat to succeed in business, sports, personal relationships, and life. This book provides the blueprint Bob has discovered for success. These are the strategies he has employed for all the years I have known him to challenge and elevate anyone who is willing to listen."

– Jared Buzzell PT, CMP
Sports Therapy and Performance Rehabilitation Manager
119 Gannett Drive, South Portland, ME 04106
Phone: (207) 661-4611 • Fax: (207) 661-4630
www.mainehealth.org

"What makes *Finding YOUR Edge* particularly engaging is Bob's ability to break down his life into digestible nuggets of wisdom. These aren't just abstract ideas or feel-good affirmations; rather, Turner uses his personal struggles, setbacks, and hard-won victories as the foundation for practical advice. His stories are candid and raw, showing that the road to success isn't always paved with wins. In fact, it's often the hardest struggles that provide the most valuable lessons. Turner doesn't shy away from sharing his failures, allowing readers to see how he turned these challenging moments into shining examples of resilience and growth.

Each chapter feels like a conversation with a mentor, as Turner invites readers to learn from his experiences and apply these lessons to their own lives. His writing is both motivational and grounded, offering real, actionable takeaways that readers can immediately put into practice. Whether you're navigating a personal crisis, seeking to push past a plateau in your career, or simply looking for inspiration to take your life to the next level, *Finding YOUR Edge* delivers.

If you're a fan of motivational books that are both empowering and practical, this is a must-read. Turner's honesty and insight will resonate with anyone looking to unlock their potential and embrace the power of perseverance. You'll find yourself deeply immersed in his stories, taking away invaluable lessons that are sure to stay with you long after you turn the last page. This book will quickly become a staple on your shelf, offering not just motivation, but a guide to turning your own struggles into triumphs.

– Ryan Brown PT, FAAOMPT
Director of Sports Therapy and Performance
119 Gannett Drive, South Portland, ME 04106
Phone: (207)661-2835 • Fax: (207)661-4630
www.mainemedicalpartners.org

"Bob Turner's *Finding YOUR Edge* is a transformative guide for anyone looking to unlock their full potential. I am always on the lookout for resources that offer practical wisdom and actionable strategies, and Bob delivers both in spades! He weaves together compelling stories, insightful frameworks, and tools that challenge you to push beyond your limits. This book isn't just a read; it's an experience that equips you to step confidently into your best self. Highly recommended for anyone serious about personal growth and performance."

– Matt Moore, Owner
Willow Brook Builders, Plainfield, NH

"*Finding YOUR Edge* is more than a book—it's a conversation with an old friend who truly understands the art of connection. This is Bob at his best: raw, real, and deeply insightful. His unparalleled ability to dive beyond the surface and bring out the best in people makes this book a must-read for anyone—no matter your business, stage of life, or pursuit of health and fitness. Every page is packed with stories, questions, and wisdom that will leave you inspired to push further, level up, and find your edge. You'll walk away with invaluable 'nuggets' that resonate long after you have finished reading."

– Stacy Cimino
Trainer, Coach, Ironman, Crossfitter, Hyrox Champion

"Bob Turner's *Finding YOUR Edge* is an inspiring guide to unlocking your potential in life and business. Drawing from his journey in the construction industry and Ironman racing, Turner weaves personal anecdotes with actionable advice on mental toughness, perseverance, and health. His authentic storytelling and practical insights empower readers to embrace challenges and discover their own 'Edge.' This book is a must-read for anyone seeking motivation and strategies to thrive in both personal and professional arenas."

– Stan Skolfield, ATC, CSCS
Owner, Skolfield Sports Performance
www.skolfieldperformance.com
Facebook: Skolfield Sports Performance
Instagram: skolfield_sports
(O) 207 602-6322 (M) 207 318-2455

FINDING YOUR EDGE

BUILDING MENTAL TOUGHNESS FOR BUSINESS AND LIFE

BOB TURNER

FOREWORD

In the world of personal transformation, some journeys stand out. *Finding YOUR Edge* is such a journey—a testament to resilience, growth, and extraordinary potential.

I'm Chris Dwyer, a mindset and personal transformation coach, and I've had the unique privilege of watching Bob Turner's remarkable evolution from a home improvement contractor to a powerful coach who transforms lives.

Bob and I first met through The Contract Fight (TCF), which helps home improvement contractors become better business people while restoring dignity to the trades. I took Bob on as a client in 2022 and was immediately struck by his character—his distinctive combination of modesty, personal and business improvement drive, New-Englander-style stoicism, abundant empathy, and genuine community orientation.

Being a part of Bob's meteoric rise to ever higher versions of himself has been a privilege and satisfaction that no words will ever adequately describe. Suffice it to say, his having become such a skilled, hands-on, life and business-oriented coach to many is both the direct result and the culmination of a whole life of having done the personal work, having created the businesses, having stepped up, fallen down and stepped up again over and over.

Ironman-style mental toughness and practical wisdom are the perfect themes for this book because Bob lives, thrives, and coaches by these themes. I've never read a book so grounded in the author's truth as this one. *Finding YOUR Edge* not only makes for an accessible, fun, and meaningful read—one that intentionally avoids needless, distracting coaching jargon and shallow platitudes—but also makes the material easy to connect with and to integrate.

All that is not to say that one can just readily adopt any mindset and instantly find themselves in a new and better reality. As Bob points out in the pages that follow, real change requires putting in the reps. So what you're about to read is more than a book. It's a psychological roadmap crafted by someone who has navigated the complex terrain of self and business development through lived experience. Bob doesn't just talk about the transformation of your life and business—he embodies it.

Each page reflects not just Bob's wisdom, but his unwavering commitment to helping others unlock their potential. *Finding Your Edge* is a beacon for anyone yearning to break through their own limitations and anyone ready to step into a more authentic, powerful version of themselves.

Congratulations on selecting the right guide—one with genuine, hard-earned wisdom to offer—for the next stage of your journey to your highest potential.

– Chris Dwyer
Mindset & Personal Transformation Coach
Beyond Mindset Coaching
The Live Limitless Community

CONTENTS

Introduction xxi

1. The Foundation of Mental Toughness 1
2. Owning Your Story 7
3. Embracing Discomfort 13
4. Cultivating Grit 19
5. Adaptability in the Face of Change 25
6. Harnessing the Power of Mindset 31
7. Victor or Victim 41
8. Building a Support System 47
9. Leveraging YOUR Edge 55
10. Unleashing Your Inner Power 63

Conclusion 79

INTRODUCTION

I'm Bailey's dad, a six-time Ironman finisher, and an entrepreneur who's spent the last twenty years building businesses and mental toughness, one tough lesson at a time. I've tried a lot of ways to reach success, but at the heart of it all, two things got me through—hard work and never giving up. And, above all, coming from a place of service. This book is here to share those experiences and help you find the mental toughness you need to level up and go after your own goals with grit and confidence.

I'll be straight with you. I've made my share of mistakes. I didn't take the traditional route of going to college and getting a business degree. My business lessons were learned on the job—doing, failing, rebuilding, and never quitting. Even when it would've been easier to work for someone else, I knew I wanted to work for myself. I never wanted to punch a clock. That approach to work—thinking like an owner—put me into leadership roles early on. I had a nose for business, and over time, I found my passion for working with people and helping them reach their own goals. That's why, in early 2023, I launched *Summit Coaching & Consulting*, and I've been running full speed ever since.

I wrote this book because I believe that if you're willing to put in the work, you can develop the kind of mindset that will let you tackle whatever life throws your way. It's my hope that these pages will serve as a guidebook for anyone who's ready to get serious about becoming mentally tough and achieving more. We all want to avoid the mistakes that hold us back, and this book offers insights to help you steer clear of the ones I've learned from firsthand.

I know that not everyone is ready to step up and do the hard work of personal growth, but if you're here, you're already different. You're already on the path to becoming more resilient, focused, and successful. It doesn't matter if you're starting late; what matters is that you're here. Developing mental toughness isn't a one-time decision; it's a daily choice. And when we show up with that intention, we're in control of how we face challenges and what kind of people we are in the process.

I've built this life with blood, sweat, and tears, and I still go into every personal development event, boot camp, or seminar, looking to come away with one thing—a tactic, a lesson, or an insight to improve myself or my business. My goal is always to find something I can use right away to move the needle forward. And that's my hope for you with this book: that you'll walk away from it with real strategies you can use and then pass along to others.

My path to becoming a coach, a speaker, a blogger, and a podcaster has been unconventional. But there's no magic pill here—just a lot of hard work. My mom jokes that the last thirty years have been my college education, to which I usually reply, "Well, why did it have to cost so much?" But I wouldn't trade that education for anything. And along the way, I found my passion. A few years ago, I was talking with a contractor who needed advice on a tough client situation. We were on the phone for over an hour, and after he thanked me, I told him to let me know how it turned out. After hanging up, I found myself pacing around, energized, saying to myself, *THAT FILLS MY CUP*. It hit me that helping people navigate their challenges was what I was made to do. I was fifty-two, and I'd finally found my purpose. Since then, I've poured 100 percent into it.

So, at the end of 2022, I decided to step into the coaching space. I had some real limiting beliefs around this decision. I questioned myself, *Who am I to be telling people how to live their lives?* After talking with friends and other coaches, people said, "Bob, you have a lot to offer. You have a lot of relatable experience. You're older than most people who step into the coaching space, and you only need to be a few laps ahead of somebody to be able to help them out." So I decided at the end of 2022 to enter the coaching world, and my mantra was: "I'm not going into 2023 without being a coach." I had to take action. I shot a video, put it out on social media, and said, "Hey, I'm stepping into this space." I told everyone what I was up to and what I was looking for, and that had to happen in order to become a coach. I had to take action, and I did. Flash forward two years, and here I am writing a book!

This book is about finding YOUR Edge—whatever that means for you. How are you showing up for yourself and the people in your life every day? Where do you go when things get hard? That's where YOUR Edge lies, and this book is going to help you find it, sharpen it, and use it to be your best.

My coach, Ben Newman, helped me uncover this. A couple of years ago, he called to say he was coming to the East Coast and wanted to meet up. Ben's one of the top five performance coaches in the world, so when he offers to catch up, you make it happen. We had a great conversation, and after listening to me talk about life, business, and coaching, Ben said, "Bob, there's an edge to everything you say. You take people to the edge." That conversation was a pivotal moment in my life. It's when I realized that I could help others the way I'd been helped—I just needed to find a way to package it. And so, *The Edge* was born.

This book will ask you tough questions, get into your business, and make you a little uncomfortable. I don't accept excuses from my coaching clients, and I won't accept yours, either. You picked up this book for a reason, and my goal is for you to walk away from it with tangible ways to become mentally tougher and more successful. Don't try to boil the ocean; just pick a few things that speak to you and dive in. Make this book your own—highlight it, mark it up, bend the pages back, and use it like a workbook.

If you're serious about growing, find someone who's already

done what you want to do and learn from them. But make it your own. There's a saying in personal development, "Your mess is your message." Now, I don't think of myself as having a mess, but I do have a message. And those who know me will tell you that I don't sugarcoat things. I'll tell you what you need to hear, not just what you want to hear, and that honesty has always brought people together. We're all pulling on the same end of the rope, and we all grow together. A rising tide lifts all boats, as the saying goes. You'll also see why it matters to surround yourself with the right people and how essential that is to staying on track.

When I first considered writing a book, I had my doubts. Who am I to put my story on paper? But then I thought about the mental toughness I've built and the stories I've accumulated— stories my friends have heard so many times they ask me to tell them again just for fun. Those stories taught me the value of hard work and resilience, and in this book, I'm sharing them with you.

When you finish reading, you'll feel more confident in your ability to go all-in on yourself. You'll see what it takes to move beyond your comfort zone, bet on yourself, and hold yourself to a higher standard. You'll have the tools to tackle negative self-talk, overcome setbacks, and push through your own limits.

Some people might say a guy who writes a book like this has a high opinion of himself. But to me, it's about self-respect and confidence. We'll talk about the difference between cocky and confident, and how believing in yourself has nothing to do with arrogance. We'll also dive into one of my favorite topics: grit. I'm a scrappy guy, and I take pride in being someone you'd want with you in the trenches. I'm the kind of guy who dives three rows deep into the bleachers for a loose ball. That's the kind of grit and resilience I want to pass on to you.

So, you picked up this book for a reason. It's time to stop making excuses, to dig in, and to go after the life you've imagined. When you close this book, you'll be ready to find YOUR Edge and take your mental toughness to a new level. Let's get to work.

CHAPTER 1
THE FOUNDATION OF MENTAL TOUGHNESS

BUILDING MENTAL TOUGHNESS: WHAT IT MEANS AND WHY IT MATTERS

Mental toughness means being able to show up for yourself and those around you, even when life throws its toughest challenges your way. It's about identifying your weaknesses, committing to improvement, and pushing through obstacles with resilience. Whether it's in business, relationships, or personal health, developing mental toughness helps us become the best versions of ourselves. For me, it's also a cornerstone in both coaching and endurance sports, where preparation and resilience are crucial to success.

In this chapter, we'll explore the mindset and practices that strengthen mental toughness. These aren't just theories but proven approaches I've learned from years of competing in triathlons, working through economic challenges, and managing teams. Mental toughness is foundational, especially when times get hard, and resilience becomes essential.

BUILDING RESILIENCE: LESSONS FROM ENDURANCE SPORT

Just like you wouldn't start a cross-country road trip without a map or GPS, developing mental toughness requires a plan. A plan provides clarity on what you want to achieve and how to get there. It allows you to set daily goals, write them down, and hold yourself accountable. As a coach, I emphasize this with clients by outlining a broader set of ten goals rather than limiting it to a few.

Stephen Covey's advice in *The 7 Habits of Highly Effective People*, "Begin with the end in mind," is essential here. Knowing the destination allows you to map the path forward with intention, instead of wandering aimlessly. Similarly, in endurance sports, it's not enough to train hard; you need to train smart, knowing where you're headed and the obstacles you might face along the way.

Resilience is essential, not only because of the challenges we face but also because everyone else is dealing with their own hardships too. One of my first triathlon coaches once told me before an Ironman race, "Look up and down the line of everyone starting today—each person has gone through something difficult to be here." That reminder helped me understand that setbacks are inevitable, but so is the opportunity to rise above them.

EMBRACING THE HARD TIMES: AN IRONMAN EXPERIENCE

In 2008, I was training for the Ironman Lake Placid, a triathlon consisting of a 2.4-mile swim, a 112-mile bike ride, and a 26.2-mile run. My training had been intense and focused, but in the days leading up to the race, I had an accident on a job site, stepping on a nail. Then, on race day, I woke up with what felt like the flu. Lying on the cold bathroom tile at 4 a.m., I could barely stand, let alone envision completing an Ironman.

Despite feeling terrible, I went down to the race to see if my condition would improve. My coach took one look at me and told me I looked awful, but I was determined to start anyway. Halfway through the first swim loop, though, it became clear that this wasn't going to be my day. The hardest part came when a race volunteer asked me for my timing chip. Removing that chip felt like handing over an entire year of training and preparation.

As I walked off the course, I saw my ten-year-old daughter, Bailey, running toward me. I held her tight and said, "Remember how I always tell you not to expect life to be fair? This is what I mean." That day, I had to make peace with the fact that setbacks are part of the journey. It's not about avoiding failure—it's about how you respond to it.

OVERCOMING ADVERSITY IN BUSINESS: LESSONS FROM THE 2008 ECONOMIC DOWNTURN

The resilience I built in sports proved invaluable in business. In 2009, during the economic downturn, my dad and I ran a small contracting business. Business was slowing, and we faced the painful decision to let go of some employees. For the first time in years, I put on my tool belt and returned to working in the field just to make it through that tough time.

One lesson I emphasize to clients is that very few people outside your immediate circle care whether your business survives five years from now. Outside of your family, close friends, or a business mentor, it's primarily up to you. Nobody is coming to save you. Adapting to change is crucial because, as I learned from the 2008 downturn, circumstances can change rapidly.

Though there were times I considered taking an easier route —maybe even getting a "real" job—it was the entrepreneurial drive inside me that kept me pushing forward. Challenges often reveal just how much more we're capable of, even when we think we're at our limit. David Goggins, former Navy SEAL and endurance athlete, often says that when you think you're done, you're only at 40 percent of your true potential. His words echo my experiences, where each obstacle showed me I still had more to give.

CULTIVATING SERVICE AND INTEGRITY IN BUSINESS

While many are motivated by money, my drive comes from creating positive experiences for my customers, fostering a good work environment, and solving problems. I see myself as a steward, coming from a place of service and understanding my clients' needs. This philosophy has helped me in both my contracting business and my coaching practice.

My business has thrived over the years not because of heavy marketing but due to our commitment to quality. When people trust you, they call you back, and that integrity builds a solid reputation. Of course, I'm not against marketing, but I believe in the power of focusing on the people in front of you—doing right by them and letting your work speak for itself.

When I started managing a custom cabinet shop in 2000, I went from being a draftsman to managing a thirty-person crew overnight. I didn't know how to build all the custom pieces we were making, but I knew how to lead the team to get the job done. My boss told me, "You may not know how to do the tasks, but you know how to motivate them to get it done." That's when I realized the importance of people skills, empathy, and supporting those around you.

CONCLUSION: RESILIENCE AS A LIFELONG SKILL

Resilience is not a skill you perfect overnight. It's a muscle you strengthen each time you encounter a setback. Whether you're training for an Ironman, running a business, or navigating life's curveballs, mental toughness and resilience are your foundation. With a plan, a supportive community, and the commitment to adapt, you can meet any challenge head-on.

CHAPTER 2
OWNING YOUR STORY

EMBRACING YOUR JOURNEY

When I was a teenager, I was that kid driving around town with a lawnmower sticking out of the back of a 1977 Chevette. From a young age, I was already learning the basics of leadership and entrepreneurship that would stay with me for life. I learned about customer service, managing money, and the consequences of not keeping my word. These were the early lessons that became the bedrock of my future endeavors.

At sixteen, I was balancing the life of a three-sport athlete, squeezing soccer practice, basketball camps, and a typical teenager's summer all into my schedule. My dad and I brainstormed ways I could make a little extra cash during my limited free time. That's how my first business idea was born: a lawn-care service, which we cleverly named Yard Busters—taking inspiration from the popular movie *Ghostbusters*. For two summers, Yard Busters taught me more than just how to mow lawns and weed-whack. I learned what it meant to make a profit, how to price my services appropriately, and the importance of delivering on promises.

One summer, my friend's dad—a successful businessman—invited me to join him and a group of about ten guys on a fishing trip up to his lake in northern Maine, just over the Canadian border. It was a remote lake, teeming with fish, and we spent the day reeling them in and enjoying the solitude of the wilderness. Later, as we gathered for dinner, I sat down, still wearing my baseball hat. My friend's dad turned to me and asked, "Bob, does your family eat dinner together at the table every night?"

Proudly, I replied, "Yes, sir, we do."

He raised an eyebrow and said, "And do you always wear your hat at the table?"

At that moment, I felt my face flush. I quickly took off my hat, embarrassed, and resolved never to make that mistake again. To this day, I take off my hat at the dinner table—even when I'm alone. This small lesson about respect and mindfulness might seem trivial, but it's lasted with me for over forty years. Those "little things," the moments we think won't matter, often do. They shape us.

Reflect on the small lessons you've learned throughout your life. Maybe there were times when you had to dig deep, show respect, or learn a lesson the hard way. These are the stories that shape us and stay with us far longer than we expect.

KEEPING YOUR EYES ON THE BALL

Another pivotal lesson came when I was in eighth grade, invited to play pickup basketball at the high school—a rare invitation that no other eighth grader received. Mr. O'Donnell, a teacher who must have been about fifty at the time, would open the gym for us. I remember his thinning hair, round glasses, and cut-off jean shorts paired with classic Chuck Taylors. This guy was relentless on defense, and the game's intensity was unlike anything I had experienced.

During a fast break, as I sprinted down the right side of the court, the ball hit me squarely in the back of the head. Mr. O'Donnell had passed it to me while I wasn't looking, and it went sailing out of bounds. Immediately, he rushed over, pointing his finger at me, and said, "Don't ever take your eyes off that ball again!"

I was mortified but grateful for the lesson. From that day on, I never took my eyes off the ball—whether it was in sports, work, or life. That single moment taught me to stay focused, stay prepared, and be ready to take action.

BELIEVING IN YOURSELF

One of the greatest lessons I've learned is the power of belief in oneself. You can set any goal, but if you don't believe in yourself, no one else will either. In 2003, I was out of shape and decided to start running and biking to improve my health. I eventually set my sights on completing a triathlon. Three years later, I crossed the Ironman finish line. That journey showed me that with commitment, consistency, and faith in yourself, you can achieve nearly anything. It doesn't happen overnight, but with the right mindset, you can push through limitations and break down barriers.

OVERCOMING LIMITING BELIEFS

We all have limiting beliefs, often ones we don't even know exist. These beliefs can stem from our upbringing, our environment, and the assumptions we make based on our background. Growing up, I wasn't particularly interested in college. I just wanted to work and make money. But because college was seen as the "next step," I gave it a shot. I tried going full-time at first but didn't enjoy it and eventually moved to part-time.

One Saturday, I found myself sitting in a sociology class, frustrated and thinking, *This isn't for me.* At the time, I had a part-time job, my own DJ business, and all I wanted was to get out there and work. I didn't fit the college mold, and that realization was freeing. While many of my classmates continued down the academic path, I built my career through hard work, persistence, and a strong belief that there's more than one way to succeed.

College isn't for everyone, and that's okay. I learned early on that success doesn't require a specific blueprint—it requires dedication, resilience, and a willingness to forge your own path.

LEARNING FROM MISTAKES

In high school, I experienced the sting of disappointment in a way that I'll never forget. As a junior, I'd been enrolled in a college-prep English course, where I excelled during the first quarter. My good grades led the school to suggest that I move up to Phase 5 English (an advanced course), which I agreed to with one condition—that I wouldn't be placed with a particular teacher. Yet, they put me in her class anyway, and out of pure stubbornness, I refused to engage. I didn't do a single assignment for that quarter, which ultimately led me to fail the class and flunk off the basketball team.

I'll never forget telling my dad about my failing grade and watching his disappointment as he took me to explain myself to my coach. My coach looked at me and simply said, "Bob, let's turn a negative into a positive." That line has stuck with me ever since. I learned that even when you make mistakes, it's possible to turn things around and find something meaningful from the setback.

"HOW YOU DO ONE THING IS HOW YOU DO EVERYTHING"

Much of what I've learned in life has been through sports—lessons in discipline, respect, teamwork, and perseverance. Years later, I still run into old friends from my high school sports days. We all laugh and reminisce, but we also recognize how the experiences shaped us. As the saying goes, "How you do one thing is how you do everything." I've come to believe in this wholeheart-edly. Every small action, every decision, and every effort reflects the kind of person you are and who you're striving to become.

Every story I've shared in this chapter—from the fishing trip to my stubborn refusal in English class—has taught me some-thing. We each have a story, a unique set of experiences that shape who we are and what we value. Own your story. Embrace it. The setbacks, the small wins, the seemingly insignificant moments—all of it contributes to the person you are today and the person you're becoming. And as you move forward, remem-ber: each story has its lesson, and each lesson is part of *Finding YOUR Edge*.

CHAPTER 3
EMBRACING DISCOMFORT

PUSHING THROUGH THE PAIN: LESSONS LEARNED FROM ENDURANCE TRAINING

Fifteen years of endurance training has taught me a lot about discomfort, particularly when to say enough is enough. I'm a "pain is temporary, but results are forever" kind of guy, yet I've learned that sometimes you need to ease up on the gas. That principle applies to both sports and business. In entrepreneurship, when you trade a nine-to-five for a 24/7, the physical and mental toll can be heavy. Similarly, Ironman training demands an extraordinary commitment, often at the expense of other parts of life. This is true for any passion worth pursuing—you start with rapid gains, but over time, as the law of diminishing returns kicks in, maintaining progress requires more and more effort. It's a tough balance, but over-doing it can lead to burnout.

Throughout this book, I talk a lot about **The Edge**. To find **YOUR Edge**, you have to go there. Remember David Goggins's 40% rule? You don't discover your limits unless you push yourself.

In 2006, my friend Mike and I decided to take on Ironman Lake Placid. We had a solid group of friends who trained together, including a few guys in law enforcement with Mike. These were fit, accomplished athletes, and though they hadn't completed an Ironman, I looked up to them. When Mike announced, "Bob and I are going to do an Ironman," they laughed and asked, "Turner's going to do an Ironman?" That skepticism was all I needed to fuel my determination.

A few months into training, we participated in a challenging sprint-distance race in Maine. The surf that day was around six feet, and two of those guys who laughed at our Ironman plan ended up being pulled out of the water on jet skis. Meanwhile, Mike and I finished the race. We went on to complete the Ironman and had an incredible experience. This taught me an important lesson: not everyone shares your dreams or believes in you—and that's okay. What matters is that **you believe in yourself**.

I like to call my shot. Some people think it's cocky; I view it as confidence. There's a fine line between the two. Cockiness is boastful, but confidence is saying, "I'm going to do this," and truly believing it.

One of the best examples of calling my shot came during

Ironman Lake Placid in 2011. In 2008, I had to quit the race, and it frustrated me—I'd trained for months and walked away with nothing to show for it. Ironman is something you can't just redo; between family and work, each race requires total commitment. So, I set my sights on 2011 as my comeback year.

I trained with a friend (another Mike), and together, we entered other races to stay sharp. Ironman was the pinnacle, and I was all in. I hired a coach, followed a structured plan, and stayed in peak shape. By race day, I was ready.

In Lake Placid, the swim, bike, and run segments are each two loops. My first loop on the run—a 13.1-mile stretch—went exactly as planned. I was running my race, feeling good, and in sync with my pacing. Mike, a skilled triathlete, was ahead of me coming off the bike, and I couldn't spot him amid the 2,600 competitors.

Heading out for the second loop, I had thirteen miles left. My parents were cheering for me from the spectator section, which gave me a huge boost. I shouted to my dad, "Where is he?" He held up four fingers—Mike was four minutes ahead. I shouted back, "He's mine!"

At that point, we'd been racing for over eight hours, and I was essentially vowing to close a four-minute gap in the middle of a marathon. But I was determined. A mile down the road, I saw another coach from Maine. "Where is he?" I yelled. "Three minutes!" he replied. "He's mine!" I shouted back, calling my shot again.

Eventually, I caught up with Mike. We ran side-by-side for about a mile, encouraging each other, but soon he started to fall behind. I decided I wouldn't look back; I'd keep running my own race. One of my mentors, Ben Newman, often says, "Don't trip on things that are behind you." I followed that advice, staying focused and hitting every water stop to get what I needed. Near the final turnaround, I saw that Mike had closed the gap, so I picked up my pace for the last stretch. I didn't want to be in a head-to-head sprint with him at the finish line.

I crossed the line forty-five seconds ahead of Mike, finishing in ten hours and forty-five minutes. After all that training and an entire day of racing, we were within seconds of each other. Calling my shot kept me focused, motivated, and accountable. Had I not made that commitment, "close enough" might have been good enough.

Remember, there's a difference between cockiness and confidence. Confidence is about setting a goal and giving everything to achieve it. Calling your shot—especially publicly—holds you accountable and pushes you to find **YOUR Edge**. I wasn't okay with "good enough." Pain is temporary, and results last a lifetime.

EMBRACING DIFFICULT CONVERSATIONS: STRATEGIES FOR EFFECTIVE COMMUNICATION

I'm a firm believer in addressing the elephant in the room. Rip off the Band-Aid; it's often easier that way. When I became more active in contractor coaching, I noticed people frequently reached out to me. One day, I asked a client, "Why did you call me?"

"You're really good at tough conversations," he replied.

I was surprised. "How so?"

"Well, you address what needs to be said without making people feel bad."

Though I didn't know it at the time, this ability to handle difficult conversations is part of what gives me my Edge. Over the years, I've developed a few key strategies that have helped me hone this skill.

One technique is **falling on the sword**. This means taking responsibility, admitting your mistakes, and being willing to say, "Maybe I didn't handle that right." When you start by taking some ownership, it helps others feel less defensive. Phrasing like "I totally understand your position on this…" can go a long way. It makes the conversation collaborative, rather than confrontational.

In my coaching calls, I often talk about not needing to win every battle to win the war. That's crucial in difficult conversations. It's about seeing the bigger picture and understanding that sometimes it's okay to let a smaller issue slide if it keeps things moving forward toward your ultimate goal.

One of the toughest lessons I've learned is the importance of listening more than talking. Years ago, someone accused me of just liking to hear myself speak. That comment stuck with me, and since then, I've prioritized active listening. This means not just hearing what's being said, but really engaging. For example, I might repeat key points back to the person to confirm that I understand.

In business, active listening is critical. I see it all the time when negotiating contracts or handling sensitive issues. If a contractor feels unheard, they're less likely to collaborate effectively.

Every experience in this chapter—from the grueling Ironman training to navigating tough conversations—has taught me the value of embracing discomfort. We don't find our true limits or discover our edge by staying comfortable; we do it by pushing ourselves, setting bold goals, and handling challenging moments with honesty and resilience. Whether it's physical endurance or a hard conversation, remember that discomfort is often the gateway to growth. Embrace it, learn from it, and use it to build the confidence that fuels your journey forward.

CHAPTER 4
CULTIVATING GRIT

PERSEVERANCE AND PRACTICE: TRAINING FOR IRONMAN AND BEYOND

My friend Jared often tells me that I have "another gear" on race day. "It just seems like you turn into a different person when the gun goes off," he once said. That got me thinking. I wasn't sure what he meant at first, so I took some time to reflect on it. Part of that reflection helped shape the concept of *The Edge* in my coaching practice. I often ask people, *What is YOUR Edge?* How do you show up each day? How do you change your behavior to strengthen your mental toughness? How do you handle difficult situations—with anger, grace, or calmness? Answering these questions helps you find YOUR Edge.

After Jared made that comment, we raced a sprint-distance triathlon in northern Maine. I knew it would require some mental toughness, so I was ready. I managed to get off the bike just ahead of him. Later, he told me that when he got to the bike rack, my rear wheel was still spinning! I wasn't far ahead, but I knew if I could get around the next corner before he saw me, I could "crack" him—an endurance term we use when someone is mentally defeated or loses their edge. Whether it was actually true or not, I used that belief to fuel my mental advantage on race day.

I try to leverage *my* Edge in every competition, whether it's an Ironman race, business challenge, or even personal relationships. If you have a mental Edge, use it—for the right reasons. You have to be gritty. You have to be scrappy. Some guys I race with say, "I don't want you nibbling at my heels late in the race because I know you're not going away." That's respect, and it honors the competition. It's a mentality of "If we're going to do this, let's do it right." To me, anything worth doing is worth doing well.

In 2010, I was competing in a Half Ironman in New Hampshire, having a strong day. I always finish with a hard push, no matter how tired I am. As I approached the final two hundred yards on a wet, grassy chute, another competitor came up on my right. I checked his calf, where they mark your age in black marker, and I thought he was in my age group. His bib said, "*Fernando from Canada*" or something like that. He wanted a sprint finish. I was exhausted, but I knew I couldn't let up with everyone watching, including my twelve-year-old daughter. So, we sprinted neck and neck, eventually collapsing across the finish line.

Chrissy Wellington, a world champion triathlete, was there placing medals on finishers. I was lying in the grass, gasping for air, when she put a medal around my neck. A bystander later asked me, "Why sprint to the finish when it doesn't really matter?" But it *does* matter. It mattered to me, to the spectators, and to my daughter. If people invest their time in you, you owe it to them—and to yourself—to give it everything you have. That's how I race: gritty, scrappy, and with respect. Afterward, I shook Fernando's hand and thanked him for pushing me to the limit.

BALANCE IN LIFE AND BUSINESS

If you're striving to do something at a high level, you're likely to find yourself out of balance at some point. People often talk about balance as a state of homeostasis or equilibrium, but the truth is, no one who has achieved greatness did so while perfectly balanced. Think of Kobe Bryant, Michael Jordan—individuals who reached elite levels by sacrificing balance in favor of intense focus. That's true in the Ironman world too.

During my Ironman years, I was certainly out of balance. I kept my business running, but I'd be lying if I said I gave it as much attention as I could have. At times, I wonder how far I could've gone if I'd put the same Ironman grit into business. But it's tough to do multiple things well simultaneously. I adopted a motto: *Never let them see you sweat.* My family was never going to bear the weight of my training, at least not overtly. I involved them when I could, and we traveled together, making the most of it. I showed my daughter what it looked like to win and lose with humility and grace.

For example, one morning, I left at 4:30 a.m. and rode a hundred miles. I was back home by 10:00 a.m., sipping coffee, when my wife came downstairs. She asked if I was going for a ride that day, not realizing I'd already returned. Balancing everything was challenging, and there were sacrifices. But the memories and personal growth were worth it.

NAVIGATING SETBACKS WITH ADAPTABILITY AND OVERCOMING BUSINESS CHALLENGES WITH TENACITY

The 2008–2009 recession was one of those times that tested my adaptability. To keep my company afloat, I went back into the field. No one knew what the economic landscape would look like on the other side. A local bank president told me that housing would likely be hit first, so we kept a close eye on market indicators. In the meantime, I ramped up our sales efforts, doing whatever we could with the limited tools we had—mailers and word of mouth.

Being self-employed comes with no guarantees. If you don't work, you don't get paid. Running a business can be humbling, and anyone who hasn't faced adversity in business either hasn't been in it long enough or isn't telling the whole story. Challenges are part of the journey, and failure isn't the end.

In 2001, I left my job to start a countertop business with a former colleague. We quickly built the business to over a million dollars in sales but needed more capital. Around that time, my partner's focus shifted, and I had to face a tough choice: close the business or try to go it alone. I ultimately decided to close, refinancing my house to settle the company's debts. I'll never forget standing in my garage, peeling the business logo off the door of my truck with a hairdryer, feeling like I'd failed. Driving through town that day felt like I had a sign on my back. But I didn't let it break me. I remembered my basketball coach's words: *Turn a negative into a positive.* I regrouped, started again with remodeling, and eventually built a new foundation for success.

Think about the times you've had to be gritty—when you faced setbacks but chose to push forward. That's grit in action. I once bought a bumper sticker at a Waylon Jennings concert that read, *This is NOT a dress rehearsal. We ARE professionals, and this IS the big time.* That's the mindset I've applied to sports, business, and life. It's about giving it everything, showing grit, and doing things others might shy away from—all while staying grounded and respectful.

When you're faced with a tough decision or a setback next week, how will you handle it? Will you take the easy route, or will you choose grit and perseverance? Reframe the challenge to something positive so you come away feeling true to yourself and the work you've put in. That's how you cultivate *your* Edge. Don't let yourself down—*this* is your Edge.

CHAPTER 5
ADAPTABILITY IN THE FACE OF CHANGE

EMBRACING CHANGE: LESSONS FROM ATHLETIC TRANSITIONS

've managed to be self-employed for the last twenty years. I'm grateful for how self-employment has allowed me to dive deep into athletics and endurance racing, but it hasn't come without challenges. Along the way, I've had to adjust and evolve, especially during times of injury or illness. Those were the moments that truly tested my patience and commitment, making me question my dedication.

In 2012, I was dealing with severe plantar fasciitis that just wouldn't go away. Eventually, I got a second opinion, only to find that the root cause was a bone spur on the top of my foot, which needed surgery. For an endurance athlete, being sidelined like that feels like a death sentence. I went through with the surgery and was on crutches for about a week. But looking back, that break was exactly what I needed. I remember asking my friend Jared, a physical therapist, "What if I raced my bike on Sunday, just seven days post-op?" He laughed but said I could, as long as it didn't hurt. I was thrilled—that was all I needed to hear. Just like that, I was back in the game.

Sometimes, though, I've had to step away not because of injury, but because things felt overwhelming. If you ever feel like you need a break, I'd say take it. In my experience, each time I took a step back for a few days, a week, or ten days, I always came back stronger. I'd wait for that spark, that moment when I'd be driving home and feel the urge to go for a run or get back to training. That's when I knew I was ready.

In endurance racing, especially Ironman, I try to embody a "slow and steady wins the race" attitude. Ironman isn't about who's the fastest—it's about who slows down the least. I learned early on that you can't rely on past victories. As my freshman basketball coach used to say, "Stop reading your press clippings." Every race, every challenge, is a fresh start.

With both my clients in sports and in business, I emphasize tracking everything—workouts, heart rate, mileage, leads, profits, or closing rates. When we can track something, we can evaluate it; when we can evaluate it, we can improve it. There's a lesson in every experience if we're open to it.

Throughout my journey, I've learned to adopt an attitude of impermanence: nothing lasts forever, so appreciate the moment. In both basketball and triathlon, I was careful not to let my identity get tied up in sports. It's easy to say, "I'm a basketball player" or "I'm an Ironman." But those aren't who I am at my core.

Over the years, I've honed core values that define who I am: character, integrity, discipline, consistency, and motivation. These values shape the kind of dad, friend, and mentor I am. The athletic achievements are just a small part of the story. I never made a living from races; I make a living by helping people and being a good person. At the end of the day, I believe that takers may eat better, but givers sleep better.

AGILE LEADERSHIP: LEADING THROUGH BUSINESS EVOLUTION

I believe that true leaders emerge in moments of adversity. That's when you see who really steps up. As the general manager of a millwork company that was acquired by a larger corporation, I had a firsthand look at how change tests leadership. After the acquisition, the new upper management wanted to overhaul how we operated, disregarding the very practices that had made us successful. Soon enough, the company became unprofitable, and it fell on me to make tough decisions.

One day, I was called into a meeting with the leadership team and told that we'd have to lay off twenty-four of our thirty employees. I knew it was going to be one of the hardest days of my life. Instead of calling each person in individually, I gathered everyone together to deliver the news all at once. These were people I'd worked with for years—many were friends who had poured their hearts into building the company from a million-dollar operation to over five million dollars in sales. If I could have left and kept a few of them on board, I would have.

That day, my goal was to lead with empathy and transparency. I knew this news would impact everyone's lives in ways that went beyond the workplace. Some were understandably upset, but I did my best to be honest and supportive. From that experience, I learned invaluable lessons about leadership: don't keep people in the dark, involve them in the big picture, and respect their capacity for understanding complex situations. You might be surprised by how much insight your team can offer, even if they're "just" punching a clock. Leadership is about recognizing each person's strengths and aligning those with the right roles.

As a manager, I held myself accountable for everything that happened within the company. If I hired someone, that decision was on me. When things went well, it was thanks to the team's hard work; when things didn't, I took responsibility. Coming from a place of high accountability is one of the most powerful positions a leader can take. It inspires trust and creates a solid foundation for future success.

I also believe in flexibility. I was never afraid to try something new, knowing that if it didn't work, we'd pivot and try another approach. As I often said, "If that doesn't work, we'll drop back five yards and punt." There's always more than one way to reach a goal.

Lastly, humility is a foundational aspect of embracing change. As a leader, it's essential to recognize that ego can be a barrier to growth. Remember, none of us are irreplaceable.

Here's a sobering visual to keep this in mind: Fill a five-gallon bucket with water and place your fist in it. Now, pull your fist out and observe how quickly the water fills the space left behind. That's how long the average company would miss you when you're gone. This exercise isn't meant to minimize your contributions but to underscore the importance of humility.

In the face of change, be open to hard work and don't fear failure. When people see you as a leader, let that honor mean something to you. Show up, make an impact, and be willing to be vulnerable and transparent. Fill the role as a steward of your company, knowing you're not irreplaceable but that you can make a lasting difference.

When you lead through change and maintain open communication, your team will believe in you and follow your lead. True adaptability isn't about avoiding challenges—it's about facing them head-on, learning from every setback, and growing stronger in the process.

CHAPTER 6
HARNESSING THE POWER OF MINDSET

THE ATHLETE'S MINDSET: STRATEGIES FOR SUCCESS ON RACE DAY

Race day is always my favorite day. I love the moment when I wake up and know I have something big to tackle that day. I love the drive to the race with a friend, talking about what we're going to do, blasting AC/DC's "Thunderstruck," and getting fired up. That's all part of my visualization process on race day. It starts long before race day. I view race day as execution day. I've already run the race in my mind—every swim, bike, and run that I've done. I visualize. If I go out for a three- or five-mile run, I'm running on the race-course (in my mind) of the next race that I have coming up. I did this mostly with Ironman because it was such a large undertaking. My mindset was the fourth sport.

Recently, I've done a lot of work on manifestation. As I read about manifestation, I laughed to myself and said, "Hey, I thought I created this," but it was really just me doing visualization and getting in the moment. I don't know if that's something unique to me or if everyone does some sort of manifestation. When I manifest, I get goosebumps. I get fired up. I'm right in the moment, so I'll be pretty calm when I get to race day and on the Ironman course. I've already been there in my mind. I can shut the brain off and just execute. Manifestation is a pretty powerful thing to be able to bring to the race. If you haven't done it, try it out. See where manifestation takes you.

For me, manifestation is my secret weapon. When I see people getting ready for the race on the morning of an Ironman, I'm looking right through them. I don't even see them. I'm laser-focused on my vision and what I need to do for the day. Many times, people ask me, "What do you do out there on the race-course for so long? You know, what do you think about? Where does your mind go?"

I've got *one* job. I always reply, "I've got one job, and that's to stay focused."

When I'm going hard on the swim, my mindset is: *I don't need my arms again today, so let's go hard.* When I'm on the bike, I'm constantly taking cues from my body. What hurts? When was the last time I ate? When was the last time I drank? How many calories have I had? How many carbs have I put in? What does my power meter say? What's my output? How far do I have to go? What's my time? Then, right back around, I ask all those questions again. I never understood when someone said they would have had a great race, but they blew their nutrition plan.

If you execute your plan, you should be right on point. I have a friend with whom I did a lot of Ironman races, and she was always very nervous on the morning of a race. She was a top triathlete world champion in her age class, but I would have a hard time being around her on the morning of a race. I love her to pieces, but I had to create a little bit of distance because I was trying to be loose and low-key and happy-go-lucky, which was part of *my* strategy. She was keyed up and worried about every little thing. I tried not to let that nervous energy in because it wasn't how I got motivated and was successful, but it was *her* plan, and it worked for her. She had a heightened sense of nervousness and chaos. She was amped up, and that kind of stuff made me nervous. In the same vein, I had to just take a step back, get in a quiet place, and get focused on what I had to do that day. It's a big undertaking to be out on the course anywhere from ten to twelve hours. The pros can complete the race in about eight hours. The real champions take the entire time allotted for the race, which is seventeen hours. That is some next-level toughness and mindset. I always try to finish before the lights come on.

Being laser-focused and putting the blinders on is important for success. One day, I put the blinders on a little bit too tightly, and it cost me. I was in New Hampshire racing a Half Ironman, which is a 70.3-mile race. It's a 1.2-mile swim, a 56-mile bike ride, and a 13.1-mile run (half marathon) at the end. It was 2013. I was in great shape. I was getting ready for Ironman Lake

Placid, where I competed a month later and had the best race ever. The day of the Half Ironman was going to be a great race for me. I had a great swim, and when I came into the bike area, I didn't see any other bikes, maybe one or two, something like that. I saw a couple of my friends on the sidelines and said, "What's going on?" And they said, "You're in the front pack!" I had never done that well in a race, so I wasted no time in transition. I was fired up and took off on the thirteen-mile run.

I ran hard. Then the guys who were 5'11" and 6'1" and about 145 pounds came to get me. I was 5'8" and weighed 170 pounds. Your weight makes a difference when you're going down the run trail. For the next hour and a half, running that half marathon, I dropped to sixth or seventh place, which was where I finished. I remember looking down at the dirt trail the whole way, and when I looked up, a volunteer waved me through. This was a couple of tenths from the finish. He didn't know I had missed the right-hand turn a couple hundred yards back, which I needed to take to finish the race. I ran up over the hill and back out onto the road. There was no one around me, and the other guys had finished, so it was super obvious to everyone but me that I had missed the turn. Everyone else was on their second loop. I was way out front. I finished the race, feeling super excited that I had the best race of my life, only for one of the competitors to say to me, "Dude, did you take a wrong turn? There was a right-hand turn back there. I think you missed it."

I said, "I did not take a right-hand turn." A wave of sadness and shame washed over me when I realized that I hadn't run the whole race. I looked down at my Garmin watch, and it said 12.99

miles, but it needed to say 13.1. I briefly considered backtracking and finishing. Instead, I went over and talked with the race director and made him aware of my mistake. He told me that I couldn't go back, and I said, "Well, you'll have to give me a DNF." A DNF in a triathlon means "did not finish." That was a tough day. That was the day that I learned that I need to be laser-focused, and I can't get blinded by the blinders.

Pay attention to what's going on around you. I hadn't paid attention at the pre-race meeting. I was laughing and joking, having fun with friends, and trying to stay loose. But a little bit of what my friend with nervous energy brings to the table would have served me well that day. I try to have honor in competition. That's part of my mindset. It helps me. Win, lose, or draw, people know that they're going to get my best. The few times that I've won, I've tried to be humble about it and make sure I do it grace-fully. When I race someone head-to-head all day and lose, I shake their hand and congratulate them on their effort. One thing that has always annoyed me is when someone says, "Congratula-tions, I didn't have a great day today." They just raced you head-to-head, but you beat them because you were either tougher or you trained harder and put more time in. But in some way, they choose to diminish your effort by saying they weren't at their best that day. I don't play like that. If you beat me, I'll tip my cap, shake your hand, and offer to buy you a beer and some pizza. Make no mistake: from start line to finish line, we are *not* friends. Everyone I race knows that. But they also know that when it's over, it's just a race, and there's a lot more to life than a winning attitude in sports and business.

Some of those same qualities that I bring to the triathlon game have helped me in business but have also cost me a lot of money. When you're not dealing with people who have the same caliber of honor as what you bring to the table, the direct effect is that it costs you money. These types of instances have also soured me on business and made me question everything. When I show up at someone's house and try to sell them a job—talking to them about a remodel, their addition, or their kitchen renovation—I always feel that I'm pretty good on my feet. I am able to connect with people. We both come away with the client feeling like they have someone they can trust. Oftentimes, people will say to me, "We're not going to call those other two guys because we trust you." After they sign the contract and I take the deposit, everything that I promised and told them we could deliver becomes an obligation.

THE TRANSFER OF TRUST

Probably the single biggest frustration for me in business is having to transfer trust. Whether it is subcontractors, employees, or vendors, transferring the trust of the customer to someone else is always a risk. It always affects me in a big way when people drop the ball. Over the last couple of years in the contracting business, I have had a steady diet of having to apologize on behalf of other people's mistakes. It is a big part of the reason I'm moving away from that business. It's what drove me to coaching. I found that I was coaching my subcontractors and saying things like, "You really should get QuickBooks," "I can't pay you if you don't give me an invoice," or "You can't send somebody to the job site that I don't know and my customer hasn't met yet." When I tell a customer that the electrician will be there tomorrow at 9:15 a.m., I don't want my phone to ring at 10:00 a.m. and the customer to say, "I thought you said the electrician was coming." Then I have to find out where the electrician is, only to learn that he had to stop at the supply house, which can be a common thing. However, the simple fact that we didn't communicate and outwardly disrespected someone's time by figuring they'd wait around for us is inexcusable (to me). The most successful people in business communicate on a high level.

These types of incidents have made me question whether I am in the right space as a contractor. All of that stuff goes against every fiber of my fabric and calls into question all of my core values. You just don't treat people that way. It makes me feel like I'm a square peg in a round hole, that this is an industry industry-wide issue, and that someone with my mindset is just going to get chewed up and spit out the other end. For a while, I blamed it on the COVID pandemic. I would say, "Since COVID, the great guys became good, the good guys became bad, and the bad guys went out the back door." I don't know why it happened, but that's what happened. In reality, I think COVID shook things out, shook things up, and it was a way of flushing out people who weren't qualified to be in the business. The unfortunate by-product of that is that all the good guys are really tired. And everybody has been operating from a place of fear, not knowing when they might get shut down again. It has changed the business climate, in my estimation, forever.

As I moved into coaching, I started working with entrepreneurs, some of them contractors. I'm leading with the attitude that I want to be the change that I want to see in the world. Put your money where your mouth is, so to speak. If you feel something should be a different way, then jump in and try to fix it. And this is me doing that. If I can affect one person, then I've been successful. If I can help one person with their business— whether it's helping them to understand their numbers, becoming a better communicator, or dealing with hard conversations—then it's a win for me. I have been winning the mindset game. To me, it's all about how you show up, what your attitude is throughout the day, even when adversity strikes, and moving forward.

THE POWER OF A STRONG MINDSET

In 2012, I was racing a sprint-distance triathlon in northern Maine. There were only a hundred competitors, so I felt like I had a pretty good chance to win. Halfway through the bike ride, I overtook the guy in first place, and I was leading the race. Five minutes later, my front tire flatted. In a sprint-distance triathlon, I don't bring stuff to change a tire. We're looking to go as fast as we can. I was looking to win it overall. These races last an hour or just under. So, if you get a flat, basically, you're out. And it was pouring rain. One of the photos I'm most proud of from a triathlon is of me walking my bike back to the transition area. I'm barefoot because I took my feet out of my bike shoes, and I'm pushing my bike in the pouring rain. There's a huge smile on my face. I don't know why I was smiling. I think I was just feeling like, *Man, I almost won that race… I could have won that race. Who knows, I might have lost it on the run.* At that very moment, I had a chance to decide what my attitude was going to be. My mindset was that I felt lucky to be there. I was on the right side of the grass. I was out here racing, and even though it was raining, I was having a blast. It didn't go my way, but be graceful about it, be classy about it. The first thing I did was shake the hand of the guy who'd won the race. So, we had a few laughs.

If you're going to win in business, you have to have a strong mindset. You have to communicate at a high level. If your communication skills are poor, work on them. Get uncomfortable. You have to have uncomfortable conversations if you're going to succeed at business. If something's bothering you, deal with it. An early rule I made was that if someone upset me and I didn't like how it was going, I would call a timeout right there and then say, "Hey, we need to have a conversation. You did this, and this is how I took it, and this is how it made me feel. Let's talk through it." Each and every time I clearly communicated how I was feeling, I came away in a better place, and so did the other person. And guess what? It was never as bad as it initially seemed.

CHAPTER 7
VICTOR OR VICTIM

CHANGING YOUR PERSPECTIVE

They say the big man upstairs only gives us as much as we can handle. Many people spend a good part of their time building their base of faith. I believe it's more of a private thing, and although I don't attend church, I respect the fact that everyone has to be at peace with their own faith. I try to be a good person, a great dad, and a friend to many. If that gets me a little closer to the Pearly Gates, then so be it. If they are saving me a chair down in the southern part of town, well, I guess there must be a reason. So, whenever I hear the Carrie Underwood song "Jesus, Take the Wheel," I picture someone just letting go, giving up, letting a higher power take control. There have been times this past year with my business where I have felt like we are driving seventy miles per hour down the road, and someone just chucked the steering wheel out the window. That's not a good feeling at all. It reminds me of a saying, "The brakes are gone, so there's no sense steering." I think we need to be careful at times how we process what life throws at us. Adversity will come, no doubt about it. Fortunately, we have a choice as to how we react.

ARE YOU A VICTIM?

Are you a victor or victim? You didn't know you had a choice, right? So much of this has to do with mindset. We have all had bad things happen to us, but are they happening *to* us or *for* us? How do we respond? Do we go on the offensive, or do we curl up in a ball in the corner and give up? Don't get me wrong, if you get drilled head-on by a drunk driver, you're probably a victim. That's not what I'm talking about here. I'm talking about reframing your mindset in a manner that has you taking a different viewpoint about the things that happened to you. If someone stopped contacting you, maybe that's a blessing in disguise. Maybe you lost your job and found a better one. Maybe you missed a great deal on the vehicle you wanted to buy, but an even better deal popped up the next week. You get more of what you focus on. Focus on the bad, and that's what you'll attract. Manifest or visualize the good over and over, and you might be surprised at what comes into your life. What current situations do you have where you can apply this shift in mindset? How can you be the victor and not the victim?

IS IT A LOSS OR A LESSON?

So many of my life's lessons have been the expensive kind. I'm not sure why that's been the case, but it always seems like what I learned has come with a price. We all make mistakes. It's part of growing up and figuring it out. However, you can take those mistakes and view them as lessons; they at least have some worth. You've heard the definition of *insanity,* right? The process of doing the same thing over and over again and expecting a different result. Learning from your mistakes can help someone else avoid making the same mistakes. That's probably the thing I've enjoyed most about coaching: being able to help someone avoid some of the pitfalls I have endured.

I always like to tell a few race stories, so here's a story about a loss and a lesson. In 2017, I trained hard for a marathon. It was my goal to qualify for the Boston Marathon. My training partners and I ran the course for the last long run, which was twenty-two miles. So, we knew the course exactly. On race day, it was pretty much a monsoon. We ran in full rain gear, so I was going to try to qualify for the Boston Marathon wearing a North Face coat. I set that aside, and we took off. We were hitting our pace even though there were probably twenty- to thirty-mile-per-hour winds and a straight downpour along the ocean in Maine.

At about the eleven-mile mark, we came upon a volunteer, and he was sending everyone to the right down a side street. He motioned the athletes to the right, saying, "Down there and turn around at the end." I knew that wasn't the course, but everyone was heading that way, so we had to make a decision and go right.

At the end of the road, there was no orange cone or anything that directed us to turn around like we usually would see in a normal race.

Everyone was turning around at the end of this little side street and then running back. We came back out onto the main course. When I hit the twelve-mile marker, my Garmin watch showed that I had run 12.5 miles. I thought, *Don't worry about it. Keep the hammer down, and they'll figure it out in the end.* I needed a 3:25 finish time to qualify for the Boston Marathon. When I hit 26.2 miles on my watch, it said exactly that: three hours and twenty-five minutes on the nose. I was just barely hanging on to an eight-minute-per-mile pace, so it took me another four minutes to finish the added half mile. The race director admitted there had been a mistake and he would do his best to fix it. The Boston Athletic Association denied his request to amend some finish times. We fell into that category. So, I had run my ass off in a monsoon only to be denied my goal, not because I didn't run well, but because someone else made a mistake. That was a loss. The lesson: life isn't fair. I kept my chin up, ran another marathon three weeks later, and tried again, but it wasn't meant to be. I went to Boston and cheered on my friends. I could have played the victim, but I didn't. That doesn't help anyone. My perspective was that I was happy, healthy, and able to drop a 3:25 marathon at age forty-eight.

Not everything has to be a loss. There's always a lesson in there somewhere. If you peel back the curtain, you can usually find the positive in every negative. The choice is yours.

SCARCITY VERSUS ABUNDANCE

I spent a bunch of time over the last year thinking about the difference between a scarcity mindset and an abundance mindset. As I have moved into coaching, I realized that some people in the same business and geographical area think it's crazy to actually have a conversation about each other's businesses. Don't get me wrong, there are networking groups where you can sit and talk about all kinds of stuff. A good example of this is Business Networking International (BNI). It's a great networking group, but they limit themselves by only allowing one company for each trade/discipline. For instance, there is only one plumber and one electrician in each chapter. That's why I really like the contractor group that I'm part of. However, it's so vast, and there are only a handful of people in my geographical area who are a part of it. Outside the group, it seems that most people have a scarcity mindset. They don't want to share business practices or beliefs or something that might help a competitor. I've always approached business from an abundance mindset. In other words, a rising tide lifts all boats. I figure if I can help everyone get better, then it just levels everyone up overall.

When I was busy in the triathlon training world, my friend Rick and I opened up a new riding center. We had the option to rent the adjacent space, but we didn't know if we would need it. As we were mulling it over, someone else came in and scooped it up. It was Scott Baumann from Iron Legion Strength Company. Rick and I kind of kicked ourselves about it, but then we moved on. I went over and introduced myself to Scott and asked him about his business. Then, I set about getting him some referrals and helping him to get his business going. Months later, he told me he was really shocked that I had handled it that way because we were looking for the same types of clients. He said that most people would have been intimidated. I never really gave it any thought. In fact, I even referred my own mom to him and his staff. Scott still tells that story to this day when he speaks to groups about business and life.

I hadn't realized it at the time, but what seemed natural to me to try to help another person can be unnatural for many others. And the bonus: I got a friend out of the deal. So, help others, and be genuinely happy when you see someone succeed. Work to level yourself up, and you'll be surprised how people respond. The best way to help yourself is to help someone else. I truly believe that. To me, it's all about mindset. Life is about choices. You get to choose your perspective, and you get to choose the mindset that you lead with. And you get to choose how you show up for others. Are you going to be a victim or a victor? Did you suffer a loss and learn a lesson from it? Do you operate with a scarcity mindset or an abundance mindset? Speaking of choices, you also get to decide if you want to play small or play big.

What is the one thing you've been thinking about doing that you haven't acted on yet? Have you ever sat there and asked yourself, *What would I do if I could do anything?* I'm talking about sitting there for ten minutes in silence, just pondering that question. Then ask yourself, *What would have to happen for me to be able to do that?* Then go do it!

CHAPTER 8
BUILDING A SUPPORT SYSTEM

THE IMPORTANCE OF COMMUNITY: FINDING STRENGTH IN RELATIONSHIPS

'm a big gatherer of people and a community builder. Both in business and sports, I've always been the guy who pulls everyone together and says, "Let's do this or that," or, "Let's do it this way or that way." For some reason, if I'm involved in something, I always end up being a key part of it, and I'm happy to take on responsibility or accountability. I've taken eighteen people to Arizona on a bike training trip and escorted people up the mountains on hikes in Maine, New Hampshire, and all over. One thing I try to do in that pursuit is to lead by example. In that process, I believe I have found my **Edge.**

At first, I thought that my Edge was more like my why. That's not the case. My Edge is what I bring to the table that others don't. My Edge is the powerful example I am to people. I really work hard as I build communities and relationships. For example, I've done this with my Facebook group, Skool Communities, and my coaching group. I've done it with my contracting business.

In being an example, I try to make my habits and disciplines bigger than anyone in my group. I think that's a sign of a true leader. I try to be the friend that I would like to have. I try to be there when people need me. There's a saying that you're the average of the five people you hang around with the most. If you hang around five millionaires, you'll be the sixth. If you hang around five bodybuilders, you'll be the sixth. If you hang around five losers, you'll be the sixth. When I'm part of a group, I focus on my "value." I ask myself, *What can I bring to the group?* and *What can I add to the group?* Instead of *What can I take from it?* I've done that with coaching groups I've joined—communities on Facebook or other social media. What do I have to add? Too often, people show up and ask what they can take. That aligns well with my philosophy of just coming from a place of service all the time. How can I help you the most? What more do you need from me? You'll be surprised what happens when you come from a place of service.

Two years ago, when I was just settling into the contracting coaching group, I noticed that guys kept reaching out to me. Maybe it was because I was older, or maybe it was because I had made more mistakes. But I found that the more time I gave those guys, the better things turned out for me. So, I just continued to do it. I leaned in and continued to make myself available, and nothing but good things have happened since.

Over the past couple of years, I've had to take a really close look at the people who I allow into my circle. I'm not saying that from an elitist standpoint. I'm coming from a "I want to protect my mental, physical, and emotional well-being" standpoint. I make people audition to get into my circle. They don't know it, but I'll ask them for something. "Hey, give me a call on Tuesday," or "Hey, would you share this post?" I try to figure out what they're made of, where they're coming from, and whether they're a person that I'd want to hike into the backcountry with. I was in Las Vegas in October, attending Ben Newman's boot camp, and I was lucky enough to hear Tim Grover speak. Tim is another top mindset coach, speaker, and mentor. He was Kobe Bryant's trainer, Dwayne Wade's trainer, and Michael Jordan's trainer. So, he's worked with the best of the best. Tim said that you must get rid of the keys and make people figure out the combination to be in your circle. Don't just give them the key. He asked who has the key to your heart, your thoughts, and your emotions. Take back the key if you believe someone is unworthy.

We all need a tribe. We need our people. We need to know where we fit. People like to be a part of something; they like to identify with something. They like to wear hats and T-shirts. So, if you are a leader and a gatherer of people, you're going to be in that position where you're providing a place for people to gather. This is how you build a community. I've enjoyed doing this. I built a community with my triathlon coaching business. I've also done it with Summit Coaching & Consulting. You may think you need to be miles and miles ahead of everybody in order to lead them, but this isn't true. You really only need to be one lap ahead. You just need to be out ahead of someone to a point where you think you can help them a little bit. And the group needs to be big enough and strong enough so everyone can still grow and achieve their goals and not want to leave.

As a community builder, I need to be raw, real, and relevant to build strong relationships. I try to be vulnerable. And if you do that with the right group, it can only help the group to grow. People need to recognize that you're a leader. If you don't consider yourself a leader but want to be part of a community, then find one that fits you. Figure out what they're doing, find out what their core values are, and make sure they align with yours.

LEADING WITH HEART: NURTURING RELATIONSHIPS IN BUSINESS AND IN LIFE

As a contractor, I never really had any sales training. In the past, I would just go out, meet people, and talk about how good a job I thought we could do. I would talk about how my guys were clean-cut and well-presented and how we did a good job on our last project. I knew nothing about sales, but I thought I knew a lot. Once I got some sales training I started to sell a lot more. I shifted my approach to asking my clients, "How can I help you the most right now?" Closing my mouth and opening my ears made all the difference in the world.

I attended a contractor event in Denver, Colorado, in the fall of 2021. It was the first time I had sought coaching for my contracting business. Whatever I wanted to tackle in life, I always sought assistance, whether it was playing the guitar, figuring out my nutrition, or succeeding at Ironman. I always had a coach, but I never had a business coach. I was excited for the conference. I was sitting in the front row, and they started talking about sales training. I sat there and kind of shut my brain off. My mentality went something like this: *Well, they're talking about sales training. I have plenty of work. I'm all set.* It wasn't until I opened my ears that I realized I had a lot to learn.

I learned so much at this conference. I learned about checking in with people on a daily basis and sending out unexpected intentional touches (UITs), essentially reaching out to present and past clients to check-in. I learned about Acts of Service and how the more I push out and give unconditionally, the more it comes back to me. I learned that there's a way to do hard things with a heart. Sometimes, people do hard things, and they just bulldoze over everybody and say, "This is the way it's going to be." I don't want to be that kind of a leader. I try to bring people into the fold and get their opinions. Finally, I learned that as a leader, it's best to give everyone some ownership and to feel like they are making a group decision.

When I was charged with managing the millwork shop basically overnight, I became the leader of thirty different people. I never realized how much people had going on in their lives until I was their boss. Part of my role was being an unofficial counselor. I'd be lying if I said I didn't enjoy it. It made me feel good.

It made me feel trusted and valued. I didn't take it lightly. People shared a lot of things with me. I tried to help them as best I could. People don't remember what you say; they remember how you made them feel. In business, you have to go above and beyond.

As a business owner, I never want to under-deliver or worry about nickel and diming my clients. The scales should always be tipped in their direction. In other words, it's important to me that they have gotten more than they paid for. Maybe that's a bit of an insurance policy against somebody saying, "I didn't really feel value in that." I want my clients to feel so much value that they will tell their friends, their neighbors, or family that they trust me. At one point, I noticed that about half of our ongoing projects were with people we had worked with before. That repeat business told me we were doing the right things. I think you would have trouble finding a customer who would use their contractor a second time. In other words, work for them again. There are so many horror stories about contractors and customers. I never wanted to be that. It doesn't mean that I, or my company, have been perfect over the years. We've certainly had our challenges, but we always come from a place of service, and we strive to be professional and better than our competitors.

If I were sitting at a client's kitchen table discussing their project and it came to light that they were talking to other contractors, I would say, "That's great. I think you should do that and do your due diligence, but do me a favor. Ask yourself this question: Could I have a disagreement with this person, sit back down at this table, figure it out, and not hate each other afterward? When the project is finished, can I shake hands at the end and have a good interaction?" That usually opened people's eyes. It's always been important to me to leave a customer/client in a better place than when I met them.

I always lead with my heart in business. It may be the reason why I'm not swimming in cash, but it's definitely the reason why I don't have bodies to step over on the way to the top. And I don't have to duck down aisle three in the grocery store to avoid someone because we didn't show up well for their project. So, build your community or become part of the community. Get with your tribe. We all need our people. Life's hard on your own. If you join a group, ask yourself what you can add to it, not take from it. If you lead people, if you own your own business, lead with your heart. Come from a place of service. Ask yourself, *How can I help this person the most right now? What more do they need from me?*

CHAPTER 9
LEVERAGING YOUR EDGE

PUTTING IT ALL TOGETHER: INTEGRATING MENTAL TOUGHNESS INTO DAILY LIFE

ver the past few years, I've made a huge commitment to personal development. Whether it be 75Hard, going to events, or attending boot camps and workshops, I've been a sponge. I've come away with a bunch of strategies to become better and get to the next level in business, sports, or life. One of the best concepts that I've learned is to just get back up one more time than you've been knocked down. We don't quit. You can always quit tomorrow. I love that one.

It never occurred to me until I was around fifty years old to prioritize self-care. It felt selfish to me. Then I realized it was actually selfless if I could better myself and show up for everyone else. I didn't know I had a choice in how I responded to something. I would just pull from whatever I had learned in training. Often, it would be a snap reaction, or I would say something I wish I could take back. Now, I will pause and take a minute. Sometimes, I count to ten. Other times, I count down from five if I have to deal with something hard. Self-care has been a huge part of it. I take care of myself, journal, reach out to loved ones, and do not let things pass me by. I've worked hard on developing strategies for resilience.

If something triggers me, I don't respond to it immediately, and I take a few minutes to digest it. In the past, I looked at this self-help stuff as a maturity thing. I used to think that I wasn't mature enough to understand the concept. But it's really a personal development thing. It's really the development of coping mechanisms that will help you deal with what you've got going on and what others have going on.

One of the hardest things I've had to overcome is not taking on everyone else's energy. I'm an emotional guy, an empath, so I feed off others' energy. Sometimes, I have to temper that. Another concept I've learned is "aggressive patience." Seems like an oxymoron, right? I'll get shiny object syndrome, whether it's a new business, something new to try, or a new activity. But I'm learning patience. Aggressive patience is always having your foot on the gas and your eyes on the prize while doing things every day that move you closer to your goal. I need to have aggressive patience with my coaching business because I'd rather snap my fingers overnight and just appear as a former contractor and a new coach. But life doesn't work that way. You have to do the work. Instead, I pour into other people and be an example of practicing what I preach.

Years ago, I started writing a blog. It was mostly about my racing exploits, things that I learned on the racecourse, and relationships I developed along the way. I didn't think anyone was reading it until I was in the grocery store one day and ran into someone I hadn't seen in a long time. They said, "Hey, I read your blog! You really write well."

I didn't know what to say. I said, "Thank you. I appreciate it. I didn't know anybody was reading it."

They said, "Yeah, absolutely, I'm reading it, and it's helped me a lot."

It occurred to me that I had a little bit of influence and wanted to lean into that. I had something more to give. That was probably the first instance of me finding my Edge, realizing that it didn't matter how good a contractor I was—I had more to give. It didn't matter how good I got at Ironman—I had more to give. And I needed to figure out the outlet for that.

This book is part of that. Working with clients every day on improving their business and life is part of that. I want to inspire as many people as I can. I want to use my relatable experiences to inspire others. As I mentioned, there's a saying in the personal development world that your mess is your message. I've never really felt like I had a mess. But I definitely have a story. Everyone has a story. I try not to be guarded. I try to be a "what you see as what you get" person. Those who are close to me and know me well know that if you ask me a question, you're going to get a straight answer. You might not like it, but you're going to hear the truth. And that's me coming from a place of service. It would be a disservice to you not to tell you what you need to hear. There may be some people who haven't liked my honesty over the years, but I believe it's gained me more relationships than it's cost me.

SUSTAINING SUCCESS: STRATEGIES FOR LONG-TERM GROWTH AND FULFILLMENT

One of my biggest struggles in business was trying to find a way to apply my Ironman intensity to the business world. For some reason, I always adjusted my intensity down. I always got more passive. I was the nice guy, as they say. That cost me a lot of money. However, I always hire people who are better than me at certain things. I have never hesitated to pay for knowledge or talent. When I first started in business, I didn't come from a framing background, but I found myself in the field needing to do some framing. I could have stumbled through it, but instead, I hired a guy and paid him more than I paid myself so that we could do a good job. The mission was that important to me.

BUILD A GREAT TEAM

I'm a team guy at the core. I've also tried to create a "never finished" culture. In other words, when we win, I look at what we could have done better, how we can do it differently next time, and where the goal is now. Simply stated, the bar is set high, so how are we going to get over it? Maybe that comes from my dad. When I was in school, I brought my report card home, feeling proud. I got an A- for a class, and my dad said, "So, looks like there's room for improvement?" He said it in a joking way, but I got the point. I've always remembered that. There's always room to be a little bit better. There's always room to adjust.

DON'T RECREATE THE WHEEL

One of the other important lessons I've learned in business is not to recreate the wheel. Find someone who's been successful at something and model that behavior. You don't need to copy it, but if it's been done before successfully, take a good hard look at what worked. Make it your own. I've seen that applied in a marketing effort where something works and works and works for years. Year after year, the same thing works. Rinse and repeat. Then I've seen business owners pivot and not do that anymore because they need something fresh. When you get right down to it and look at what is going on behind the scenes, you may ask, "Why did you stop doing that?"

The response you may receive: "Well, we did that for years and years and years."

You: "Why don't we just do that again?" That's why I make the big bucks.

DON'T LEAVE THE BUSINESS TOO EARLY

I think a lot of people think they need to separate themselves from the business, and they wind up doing it too early. For example, an electrician or a plumber wants to come out of the field because they want to run their own business. I've seen people (myself included) leave too early. It needs to be a stepped approach, such as coming out of the field for one day more than usual. And then, in a few months, when things are still going smoothly, pull out of the field for another day and slowly transfer into being the guy who's working *on* the business instead of *in* the business. I've seen guys make wholesale changes and have to jump back into the field to straighten everything out. The reason for this is typically because they didn't have the necessary processes and procedures in place before they made that change. Make sure everything's running smoothly before you do that.

When leveraging YOUR Edge, I think it's important to do a few things. First, identify your biggest strengths and your biggest weaknesses. It's taken me a long time to realize or get behind the fact that we all need to work on our weaknesses, but why not play to our strengths? I've mentioned it before, but I don't ever want to be a QuickBooks expert. I don't ever want to learn how to create a funnel. I don't ever want to learn how to create a website. I want to play to my strengths. I want to meet new people. I want to have new discussions. I want to create new communities. I want to write another book, start a blog, and host my podcast, *The Summit*, where I interview top performers. I also want to bring on a new client and help someone figure out a plan to get through some hard things. Those are my strengths. Why would I not work on those? Ask yourself where your biggest opportunity to improve is. Pour your energy into that. What are the things you need to focus on in order to make that happen?

And lastly, what needs to go away? What have you been doing that's not working? What do you continue to do just because you've always done it that way?

When I consult with business owners and ask, "Why do we do this? Why do you do that?" they often say, "We've always done it that way." That is *not* a good answer. You need to have a different answer than that. If you're doing something because you've always done it a certain way, that's not a good enough reason. Lastly, be sure that everything is always in play. Don't be so steadfast that you wouldn't consider changing it. You didn't invent business. There is more than one way to go about accomplishing something, more than one way to get something done, and a million different ways to be successful. Have an open mind and be willing to change.

CHAPTER 10
UNLEASHING YOUR INNER POWER

SELF IMPROVEMENT

The journey of self-improvement over the past few years has been eye-opening for sure. I've learned how to sell, communicate, and resolve conflict. Confidence and self-esteem are vital components of personal well-being and success. They tend to shape our interactions, decision-making, and overall outlook on life. However, for many of us, building and maintaining a healthy level of confidence and self-esteem can be a challenge. Be honest, stay raw, real, and relevant. No bullshit, be kind to yourself. I constantly reflect on what's working and what's not. In this chapter, we'll explore effective strategies and practical tips to boost confidence and self-esteem and develop a positive self-image.

BUILDING CONFIDENCE AND SELF-ESTEEM

I think a lot of people struggle with confidence and self-esteem. If you don't believe in yourself, how can you expect someone else to? So much of what we are able to accomplish in life is rooted in how we feel about and speak to ourselves. If you're not careful, that kind of stuff can get away from you, and you can talk yourself right into a rut. A lot of times, I wake up between 2:30 and 3:00 a.m., and I fight the self-doubt for a while, but then I throw in the towel, hook up the coffee IV drip, and start writing. I'll usually pay for it later in the day, but for the most part, that's when I'm most creative.

If you're highly confident but respectful, there's nothing wrong with that. Now, don't get me wrong. If you're in a competitive situation with me, I'll probably talk more trash than Larry Bird did in the 1980s when he was on the Celtics. But it comes from a place of fun and gamesmanship. I guess people who misread me would interpret that as arrogance. I don't spend a lot of time thinking about it, but it did spark my interest enough to include it in this book.

As for the "arrogant" comment… Well, I can kind of understand where that comes from. I've put myself out there in a big way over the past couple of years: videos for my contracting company, shooting *The Summit* podcast, starting Summit Coaching & Consulting, and going all in on social media with regard to building that. Add to that group coaching, motivational speaking, YouTube, Instagram, Facebook, TikTok, you name it, all in pursuit of helping others. If that's the definition of arro-gance, then sign me up.

EMBRACE SELF-ACCEPTANCE

Do you like yourself? The first step toward building confidence and self-esteem is embracing self-acceptance. Acknowledge your strengths, weaknesses, and imperfections. Embrace your unique-ness and realize that nobody is perfect. I've heard it said that we should find our uniqueness and exploit it in the service of others. Remember that self-acceptance doesn't mean complacency but rather a foundation for growth and self-improvement. Have you ever spent significant time alone? From time to time, I head up to my camp in northern Maine by myself. At first, it was really strange, but I've grown to enjoy the time. Don't get me wrong, I love having people around, but getting comfortable with being by yourself is not a bad thing. Learn to like that person you are hanging out with. Give that person in the mirror some grace, understanding that they (you) are doing their best.

CHALLENGE LIMITING BELIEFS

Identify and challenge the negative beliefs and self-doubt that hold you back. Replace self-defeating thoughts with positive affir-mations. For instance, "I am" statements have been very effective for me. For example, "*I am* a sought after speaker coach."

Reframe your inner dialogue and focus on your accomplishments and potential. Surround yourself with supportive and positive influences that reinforce your belief in yourself.

If my coaching client runs up against a limiting belief, I'll ask them, "What would have to happen?" In other words, when someone feels as if they can't get to a certain level or are not worthy, I insert my question, "What would have to happen in order for that to change?" That's when things get real, and we're able to figure out the limiting belief. Once we have identified it, we can attack it with positive affirmations and "I am" statements.

SET MEANINGFUL GOALS

Setting and achieving meaningful goals can significantly boost confidence and self-esteem. Start with small attainable goals and gradually progress to more significant challenges.

Celebrate each accomplishment along the way as it reinforces your belief in your capabilities and strengthens your sense of achievement. Many people seek out an accountability partner or attempt to put the responsibility of attaining their goal on someone else. Before you do that, take some time and be accountable to yourself. Honor your commitment to yourself and your own well-being.

We talk a lot about SMART goals in my Edge community. **SMART** is an acronym. **S=Specific, M=Measurable, A=Attainable, R=Realistic and T=Timely.** You will have more success at achieving your goals if they are SMART. Instead of saying, "I want to do a triathlon," be more specific and say, "I'm going to do a sprint-distance triathlon on July 15." I'm going to lose fifty pounds versus I'm going to lose five pounds, and then I'll do that nine more times. If you have a goal, run it through this acronym and make sure it checks all these boxes.

In 2005, when I decided to do the Ironman in 2006, I wanted to set some specific goals. It wasn't just going to be, "Let's go race and see what happens." That wasn't good enough for me. So Mike and I sat down and talked about what we wanted for our goals. Obviously, the biggest goal was to finish the race, so that was goal number one. We got a little bit more specific and said that goal number two would be to finish in under twelve hours. That's pretty specific. I don't know if Mike's third goal was to beat me, but my third goal was to beat Mike because we had a healthy, competitive relationship full of camaraderie and genuine friendship. However, when the gun went off, we were going at each other pretty aggressively.

This is an example of setting SMART goals. My goals are specific and meaningful. Yeah, I wanted to finish Ironman, but I also wanted to do well. I wanted to finish in under twelve hours. I also wanted to beat my friend. So when race day came, we both had a great day. We finished in under twelve hours, and I beat Mike for the first time ever. If I hadn't set those meaningful goals, I don't think I would have kept my foot on the gas. I could have been out there saying, "Well, I'm going to finish in under twelve hours; that's good enough." But when I knew that was in hand, I started looking around for Mike and said, "Where is he, and can I beat him?"

CULTIVATE SELF-CARE

Self-care is essential for nurturing confidence and self-esteem. Prioritize activities that promote physical, mental, and emotional well-being. Engage in regular exercise, eat nutritious foods, get sufficient sleep, and engage in activities that bring you joy and relaxation. In other words, do things that make you happy. Taking care of yourself sends a powerful message of self-worth and reinforces a positive image. Be squared away. Do the little things that matter. I have made my bed for 2,982 days in a row. Does it matter? It matters to me. Taking care of yourself takes effort.

SURROUND YOURSELF WITH SUPPORTIVE PEOPLE

Surround yourself with individuals who uplift and support you. Put some distance between you and those who don't want to see you succeed. Seek out relationships that encourage your growth, provide constructive feedback, and believe in your potential. Distance yourself from toxic relationships that undermine your confidence and self-esteem. Join communities or support groups that share similar goals and values. I have created relationships with a bunch of great people over the past few years just by jumping into trade organizations or coaching groups. Get around the right people. Get in the right rooms. You'll be amazed at the shift in your perspective. Everyone needs a tribe. In business, I kind of always went at it alone. I never realized there were people who were struggling with the same things that I was.

In 2021, I was listening to *The Contractor Fight* podcast about contracting. They were having an event in Denver in September of 2021. After a couple of weeks of thinking about it, I decided to register for the event. When I got to Denver, I walked into a banquet room of three or four hundred people. Many of them already knew each other, but I didn't know anyone. It took a lot for me to step out of my comfort zone to go to this event. But afterward, I came away with three to four hundred new friends who were all pulling on the same end of the rope as me. I remember saying to a few of the coaches in that group, "You guys are going to be in my life." And they still are to this day. They're the right people to have around me. Surround yourself with people you can turn to when the shit hits the fan. If you bring in those kinds of people in your life—people who challenge you and don't take your excuses—you'll end up just organically dropping the people who don't enrich your life.

STEP OUT OF YOUR COMFORT ZONE

Pushing beyond your comfort zone is a powerful catalyst for personal growth. Embrace new challenges and embrace the unknown. By stepping into unfamiliar territory, you'll discover hidden strengths and capabilities, which, in turn, will enhance your confidence and self-esteem. As I mentioned, you are the average of the five people you spend the most time with. Take a look at your five. Who are they? What are their habits?

Don't be afraid to get uncomfortable. Over the past two years, I've been doing some public speaking. Because of my years behind a microphone as a DJ/MC, I don't usually get nervous to get up in front of people. However, it can still be uncomfortable, and I still force myself to do it. Every time I do, someone comes up to me and says they are glad I did it, and they take something away from it. That fuels me to do more. Over time, I have become more comfortable with it.

I got uncomfortable at the end of 2023. I had dinner with Ben Newman, my coach, in Foxborough, and he challenged me to organize an event, a personal development day. I viewed it as a large event, with two to four hundred people, and I had no idea how to pull together this behemoth of a thing. I scaled it down, set the date, and told Ben, "We are doing this." I made it manageable, but it was still uncomfortable. I had no idea what I was doing. I reached out to friends and family and got a lot of help.

On January 12, 2024, we kicked off The Edge event. I had reached out to several speakers and invited them to speak at my event, and they agreed to participate. The speakers inspired people, challenged people, and motivated them to get out of their comfort zone. It impacted a ton of people, and it helped them get uncomfortable. Toward the end of the event, I just stood back in the corner and allowed myself to feel good about what I had created. But I had to become uncomfortable to do it. It's easy to sit back and say, "Well, you know, I don't need to do that. Everything's fine. I don't want to complicate my life," but if you get uncomfortable and you do the thing, the sky is truly the limit.

CELEBRATE YOUR ACHIEVEMENTS

Acknowledge and celebrate your achievements, no matter how small they may be. Take time to reflect on your progress, and don't downplay your accomplishments. Celebrating milestones reinforces a positive self-image and your belief in your abilities. It can be a slippery slope to always be striving for more. There's nothing wrong with stepping back, taking a breath, and sitting with your accomplishments for a few minutes from time to time. You're doing just fine. I've got a lot of medals from doing races or triathlons. I never understood why people throw them in a box and forget about them. To me, they trigger great memories and are a representation of a lot of hard work. I hang mine up, and sometimes, when I'm struggling, I look at them and know that I'm doing all right. It's not a flex. Many of my friends have five times the accomplishments that I do.

I talk a lot about my Ironman exploits and achievements, as well as stories from my Ironman days and all that stuff. Someone pointed out to me recently that, on paper, I'm a multi-time seven-figure entrepreneur. I just kind of laughed and said, "Well, where are the seven figures?" But it occurred to me that I *have* done a lot of things. I *have* had a lot of success. Sometimes, when we're not where we want to be, or we haven't reached our own summit yet, we don't give ourselves credit for the peaks that we reach along the way. The truth is, I have been involved in the creation of multiple seven-figure businesses worth a million dollars or more several times, so I know how to do it. And it's okay to say that because it's the truth. So don't hide from your achievements.

It doesn't have to be boastful, but when someone asks you what you've done and what you've accomplished, don't bury the big stuff.

PRACTICE SELF-COMPASSION

Be kind to yourself and practice self-compassion. Treat yourself with the same level of care and understanding you would extend to a loved one. Accept that setbacks and failures are a natural part of life's journey and use them as opportunities for learning and growth. Cultivate self-esteem. Respect yourself. You can't command the respect of others if you don't have a high level of respect for yourself. You would never speak to someone the way you speak to yourself with your inner dialogue. Recognize when you need to cut yourself some slack. Look sharp and do your best to have a solid, personal presentation. It matters.

In 2024, I decided not to consume alcohol. Not for any particular reason. Not because I had a problem. Just because I felt like it was something that I could control. All too often today, we're faced with things that get away from us. Things that control our day. Things that hijack our day or week. There have been times in my life when I've struggled with my weight, injury, lacking motivation, or procrastination. Sometimes, I felt like those things weren't in control. This year, I decided that I could control what I consumed. Of course, there have been times when I wanted a drink or a beer with dinner or at a social event, but I've gone without, and it didn't kill me. It's also a great feeling to go to the doctor for a checkup, and when they ask you how many drinks you have per week, it's fun to say "zero."

CONTINUOUS LEARNING AND PERSONAL DEVELOPMENT

If I told you what I've spent on personal development since 2021, you would be shocked. But when I walked into Denver for *The Contractor Fight* event in 2021, I had never spent a red cent on anyone to help me with my contracting business. I've spent the last few years working on myself, and oddly enough, even though it's helped me improve my contracting business, it ignited a fire in me to become a coach. The fire that has been ignited in me is not going out anytime soon. Along the way, I've met some great people. I met Ben Newman, one of the top 5 performance coaches in the world, and recently completed his coaching certification program.

In a few short years, I've gone from being a contractor to a certified coach! Now, I'm creating personal development relationships with friends. I have literally changed the makeup of everyone around me just by being willing to commit to continuous learning and personal development, something I had no idea about five years ago. Commit to lifelong personal development and learning. Expand your knowledge, acquire new skills, and pursue your passions. Engage in activities that challenge and inspire you, fostering a sense of purpose and accomplishment. The pursuit of personal growth fuels confidence and self-esteem. Do some things that scare you. We only get one trip around this track called life, and none of us are getting out of here alive. Make an impact. One of the most interesting things I learned about my personal development journey is that we are never done. There is no finish line. There's always something else to work on and get a little bit better at—another level to attain. Ask yourself how you're showing up for the people in your life. Could you be doing better? Give people your best. They deserve it.

PRACTICE GRATITUDE

Gratitude is a powerful practice that cultivates positivity and self-appreciation. Take time each day to reflect on the things you are grateful for, including your personal qualities, achievements, and people who support you. Cultivating gratitude helps shift your focus from self-criticism to self-appreciation, enhancing your confidence and self-esteem. Pay attention to where your energy goes. I've been focusing on that a lot lately. One of my favorite sayings lately is, "I don't have the bandwidth for that right now." It's a convenient way of saying that I'm focusing on other things, but it's also a safeguard that I'm not letting things in that don't deserve my headspace. One thing I say a lot to people now is, "I appreciate you." I don't simply say thanks. Before I hang up the phone, I will tell my friends, "Hey, I appreciate you." It's one of the last things I say to people all the time. I'm not looking for anything in return. I just say it in the hopes that maybe other people will say it as well. I've always felt that I was thankful for everything, but if you don't practice gratitude—if you don't say it—it's awfully easy to just cast it aside and make an assumption out of it.

GET A LITTLE MORE SELFISH

Did I just say that? Yes, I did. Don't be afraid to do some things for *you*. You don't need to be last. In fact, the more you make your own health and well-being your number-one priority, the better off you will be and the healthier you can show up for others. So is it really selfish, or is it self*less*? In the end, the opinion you have of yourself is the only one that matters. It is cliché to say this, but what others think of you is none of your business. It truly is not. Do what makes you happy. Stand up a little straighter. Walk a little bit taller. You are doing good things, and gosh darn it, people like you.

SAY *NO* MORE OFTEN

What are you saying yes to? We all have a lot of demands on our time and energy as we get older. Our time becomes more valuable because we're spending a lot of time developing our careers or making ourselves available for our families. If we are in the habit of always saying yes to everything that is asked of us, it can become very overwhelming. Ask yourself this, "When I say yes to things that don't deserve my time, who pays the price?" If the answer is your kids, family, friends, and yourself, then take a look at what you are saying yes to. It's okay to say no. Save those "yeses" for the right situations. Someone always pays the price when you say yes. Determine who that is, and it's a little bit easier to say no.

Lastly, when you say no to something that is not worthy of your time, you get to say yes to something that is. I get invited to a lot of things. Over the past couple of years, I've said "no" a lot. I'll get invited to day drinking, to brunch, going out on Thursday night, having a couple of beers at bowling night, you name it. Hard pass. My barometer for whether I want to do something like that or not is this. If it doesn't move the needle or move me closer to my goals, it's a hard no. A no, no, no. However, I don't want to offend anyone. I also want to keep the relationship door open so they won't forget about me. The best way to say no is, "I wish I could." It doesn't have to be a no forever. It's a "not right now." For instance, I just wiped Ironman Lake Placid off my calendar this year. It's not right now. My training hasn't lined up. I've had some injuries. And I found that it was stressing me out to the max trying to get my training in, so I wiped it off the calendar. And that's okay. It'll be there when I'm ready to go back. So don't be afraid to say "No," "Hey, I wish I could," or "Not right now."

EMBRACE SELF-ACCEPTANCE

A couple of years ago, I was really struggling with what I wanted to do for work, life… everything. Every Thursday or Friday, I would ask myself *What do I want to do this weekend?* I felt like I had been doing what everyone else wanted me to do all the time. In the process of putting myself first, I became a little bit selfish.

I asked myself what I wanted to do this weekend, and for eight weeks in a row, I went to my camp in northern Maine and trimmed back trees on the road. I ended up trimming back about 1,600 feet of road over the course of eight weeks and made two dozen brush piles the size of a truck. But that's what it took to get me where I needed to be. It was a great time to reflect, to accept where I was, who I was, and just be. It's hard to focus on anything else when you're running a chainsaw, so that's why it was a great activity for me to get out and do something by myself. It was nice to take some time to think about where I was and where I wanted to go.

So there you go, a bunch of different ways to build self-esteem, confidence, and embracing everything positive to help you move forward in life with a good attitude and an open heart. It starts with you. Live your life. We only get one. Don't waste it.

CONCLUSION

THE JOURNEY AHEAD

CONTINUING TO REFINE YOUR EDGE

Thank you for taking the time to read this book. This is literally an example of me walking the walk, getting uncomfortable, coming from a place of service, and doing hard things. It took a lot of time. It took a lot of thought, stories, and examples of when I encountered moments of truth, opportunities to be mentally tough, and instances when I needed to sharpen my Edge to get to the next level. As I mentioned, I hope you're able to take a nugget or two of useful information from this book and apply it to your own personal development journey—something that helps you sharpen **YOUR Edge**. Maybe there's a voice in the back of your mind that won't let you settle for less than you're capable of. Maybe you've changed the negative self-talk to positive affirmations, and you're now celebrating your wins.

You're now reaching out to people and showing up differently and from a place of service.

This personal development journey is never finished. We are always working on ourselves. As you've read through this book, have you thought about the one thing that you have never had the courage to do? Whether it was to reach out to a certain person, start a business, or kick off that side hustle. So, I'll ask you again. What would have to happen for you to go all in on you? What would have to happen for you to step out of your comfort zone? You see, time is going to go by whether you do these things or not. They're not making any more of it. We get twenty-four hours every day. This is a short trip we're on. What do *you* want? Where do *you* want to be? You've reframed the word *selfish* into *selfless*. You now know that it's okay to work on *you*. It's not selfish.

The better you show up for yourself, the better you should show up for everyone else in your life. I would guess that if you're reading this book, you're probably already leading people in some way, whether it's your family, your business, or you're a high performer at work. Again, don't try to boil the ocean. Take a couple of things and apply them to how you go about life going forward. Get around the right people and move away from the people who don't help you move the needle. Now, that doesn't mean you have to call people and say, "Hey, we're not friends anymore." Instead, turn the dial down on how much you interact, what you say yes to, and how much you invest in things that aren't moving the needle for you. Remember to always ask yourself, *If I say yes to something, what is it that I'm effectively saying no to?* Who gets less of you because you said yes to something that doesn't move the needle? Hold yourself to a high standard.

Journal. Read books. Move your body. Eat nutritious foods. Get to bed on time. Treat yourself the way you would want to be treated or the way you would treat someone else. Lastly, find your tribe. Seek out a community. When I trained for Ironman, I would jokingly say that misery loves company. This isn't that. This is you getting in the right rooms. If it takes attending an event, do it. Get around the right people.

Don't be that person leaning against the wall, being a wall-flower, waiting for someone to introduce themselves to you. Get around a community or build a community if you need to. If you can't find one, build one. That's exactly what I've done. I built a community as a Skool group. It's called The Edge, which is no surprise, I'm sure. If you'd like to become part of our community, scan the QR code at the end of the book. You can also join our free Facebook group, The Summit, where we post positive things on a daily basis. Be around people who are like-minded. They say if you want to go fast, go alone, but if you want to go far, go together.

As part of that, I've also created a small group coaching platform called The Peak. It's a smaller, more intimate group where we do group coaching for entrepreneurs and intrapreneurs to get better at life and business. If you'd like more information on The Peak, you can scan the QR code on the next page.

One of the things that impacted me most, and what my coach, Ben Newman, said to me is this: "Let me know what more I can do for you." I've tried to employ that in my own coaching and simply come from a place of service. I'll say it again: The more I push out, the more I help people, the better things seem to get, and the more opportunities come my way. You can't truly have a great day until you've done something for someone else without looking for something in return. Take something from this book and apply it. Join our community if you so desire. Post your wins and post your losses. We'll help you celebrate the wins and absorb the losses. I hope you value the time you spent reading this book and that it has a lifetime of impact on you. When I was a kid playing middle school soccer, my coach said something just before the game started that has stayed with me all these years, and I'll leave you with it. He said, "All right, guys, lace 'em up tight and take no prisoners." Go forth and conquer, my friends.

LFG.

If you'd like to become part of our community

SCAN THE QR CODE:

SCAN ME

THANK YOU FOR READING MY BOOK!

Just to say thanks for buying and reading my book. I would like to offer you a free 30-minute strategy session!

Scan the QR Code:

I appreciate your interest in my book and value your feedback as it helps me improve future versions of this book. I would appreciate it if you could leave your invaluable review on Amazon.com with your feedback.

Thank you!

www.ingramcontent.com/pod-product-compliance
Lightning Source LLC
Chambersburg PA
CBHW070054100426
42740CB00013B/2841